EP Biology Printables: Levels 5-8

This book belongs to:

_____

This book was made for your convenience. It is available for printing from the Easy Peasy All-in-One Homeschool website. It contains all of the printables from Easy Peasy's biology course for levels 5-8. The instructions for each page are found in the online course.

Easy Peasy All-in-One Homeschool is a free online homeschool curriculum providing high quality education for children around the globe. It provides complete courses for preschool through high school graduation. For EP's curriculum visit allinonehomeschool.com.

EP Biology Printables: Levels 5-8

ISBN: 9798621542276

First Edition: July 2019

Label the Skin

9/25

Label the skin using the words in the box.

~~sebaceous gland~~   ~~dermis~~   ~~sweat gland~~

~~subcutaneous~~ tissue   ~~epidermis~~   ~~hair~~

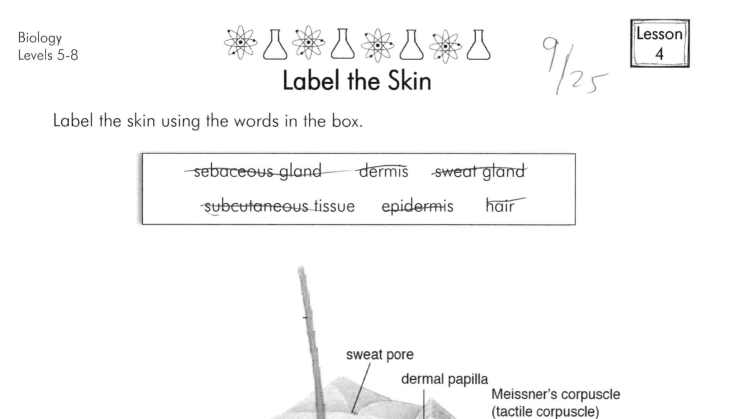

sweat pore

dermal papilla

Meissner's corpuscle
(tactile corpuscle)

stratum corneum

pigment layer

Epidermis

stratum germinativum

stratum spinosum

stratum basale

Dermis

arrector pili muscle

Oil glan

Tissue

Hair

nerve fiber

blood and
lymph vessels

vein

artery

Sweat gland

Pacinian corpuscle

Skeleton

Label the skeleton with the name of each bone.

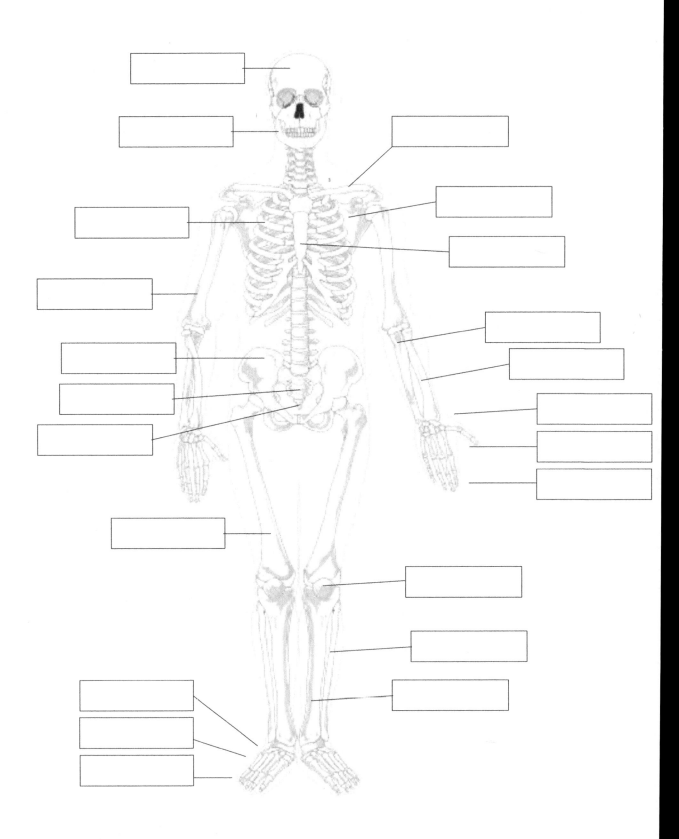

Digestive System

Label the digestive system. Use the word box to help you.

esophagus liver rectum appendix stomach
pancreas small intestine large intestine gallbladder

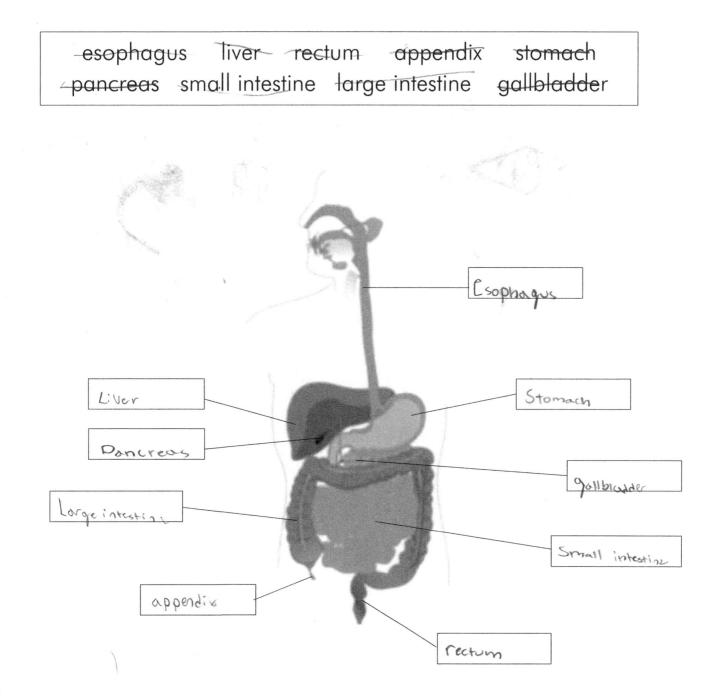

Esophagus

Liver

Pancreas

Stomach

gallbladder

Large intestine

Small intestine

appendix

rectum

Word Search

Find the skin words in the word search.

```
N O S Q R I D L E J R R T G
R M S E H F O L L I C L E S
L N U F G Y H H N C O L M I
L I O N R L L E I O U H Z M
D K E H I Z A I Z C U D B R
R S N K N H R E V M E V E
E T A E W S A A N S W R R D
R X T R W T U L S U H M O I
O I U S N M U T E Z S I D P
P D C J P M X S V M Z S N E
I U B J R I A H R J G X I F
Y S U D M Z G S E S R F Z Z
A A S X R E Y C N W K U T Q
O P T X J L L E C V B A G X
```

cell   dermis   epidermis
follicle   hair   melanin
nerves   pore   skin
sweat   subcutaneous

Label the Muscles

Label the muscles using the words in the box.

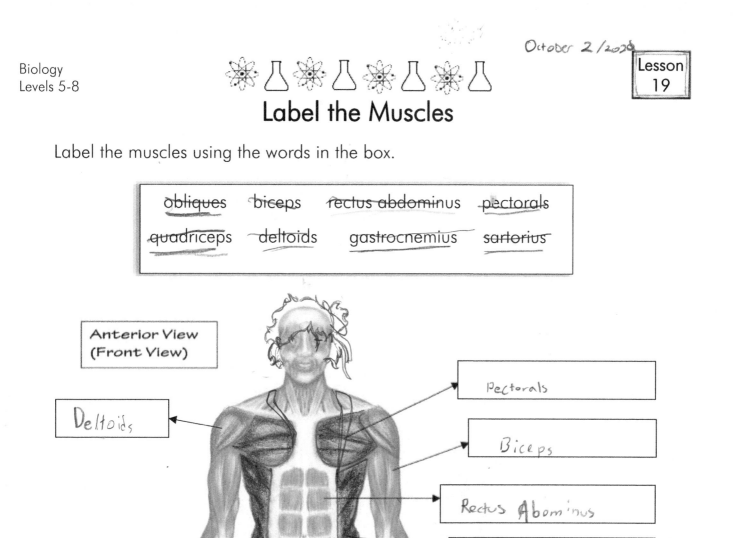

obliques   biceps   rectus abdominus   pectorals
quadriceps   deltoids   gastrocnemius   sartorius

Anterior View
(Front View)

Deltoids

Pectorals

Biceps

Rectus Abominus

Obliques

Sartorius

Quadriceps

Gastronemucis

Quads
• Hamstring curls

Gastro
• Dumbell jump squat

Label the Heart

Label the heart using the words in the box.

| right ventricle | left ventricle | pulmonary vein |
| right atrium | left atrium | pulmonary artery |

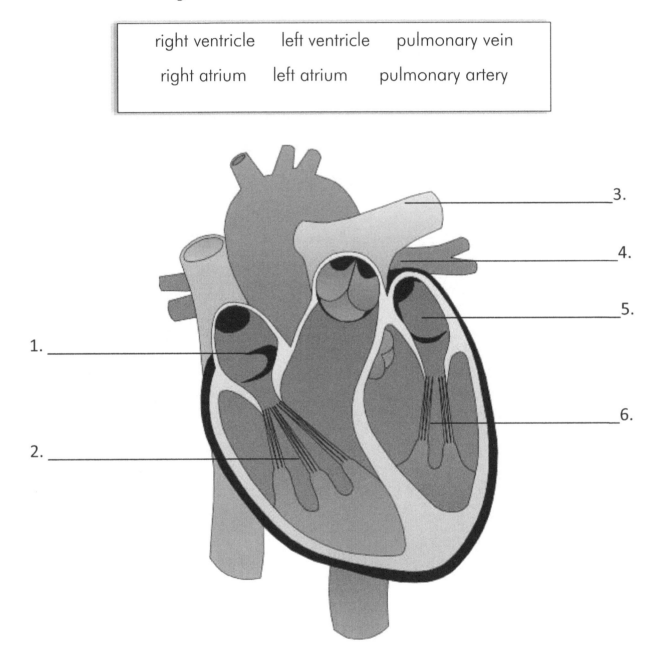

3. _____

4. _____

5. _____

1. _____

6. _____

2. _____

Label the Body

Label as much of the body as you can.

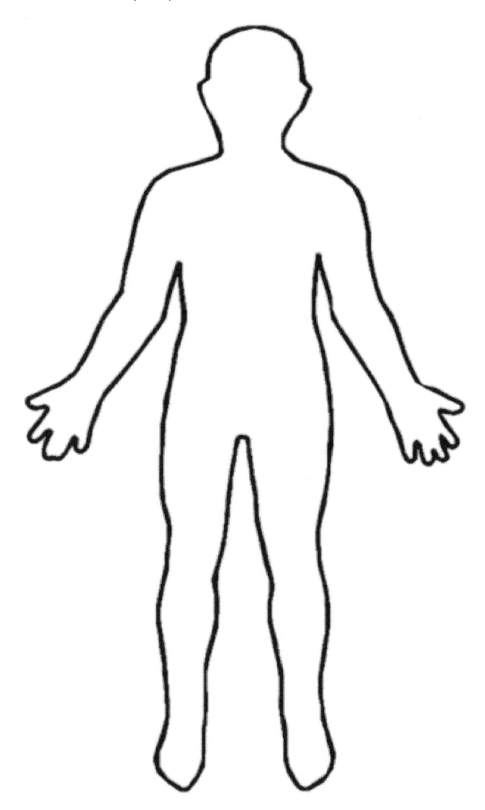

Label the Lungs

Label the lungs using the words in the box.

alveoli	bronchioles
bronchus	trachea

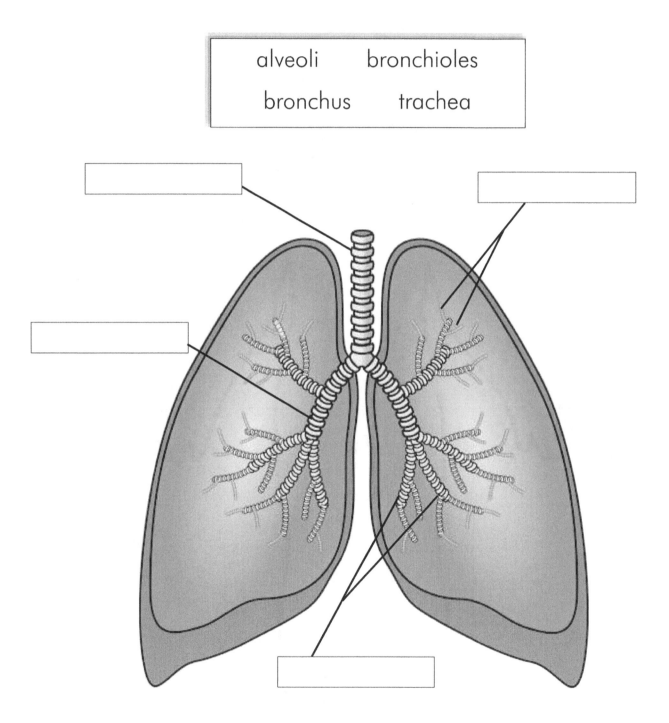

Label the Nerve

Label the nerve using the words in the box.

| axon | axon terminals | cell body |
| dendrites | nucleus | myelin sheath |

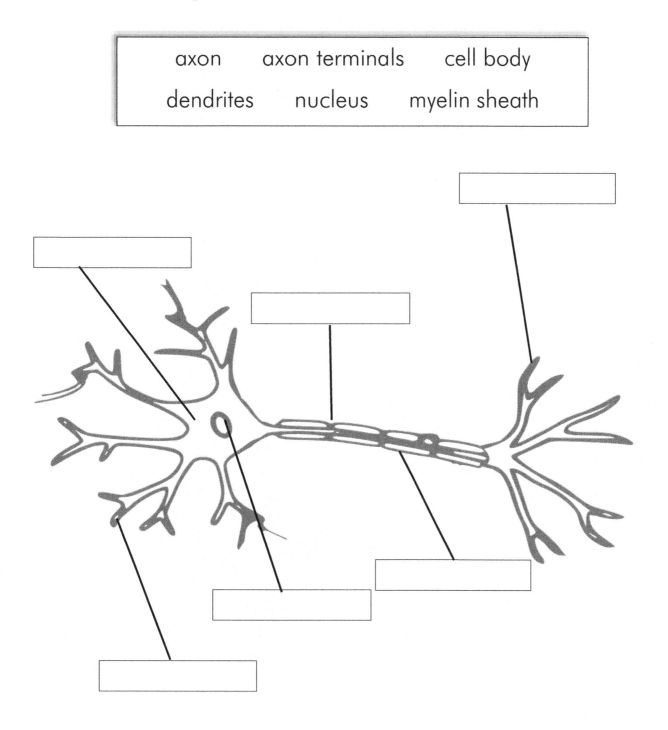

Lesson
41

Label the Brain

Label the brain using the words in the box.

| brain stem | cerebellum | frontal lobe |
| occipital lobe | parietal lobe | temporal lobe |

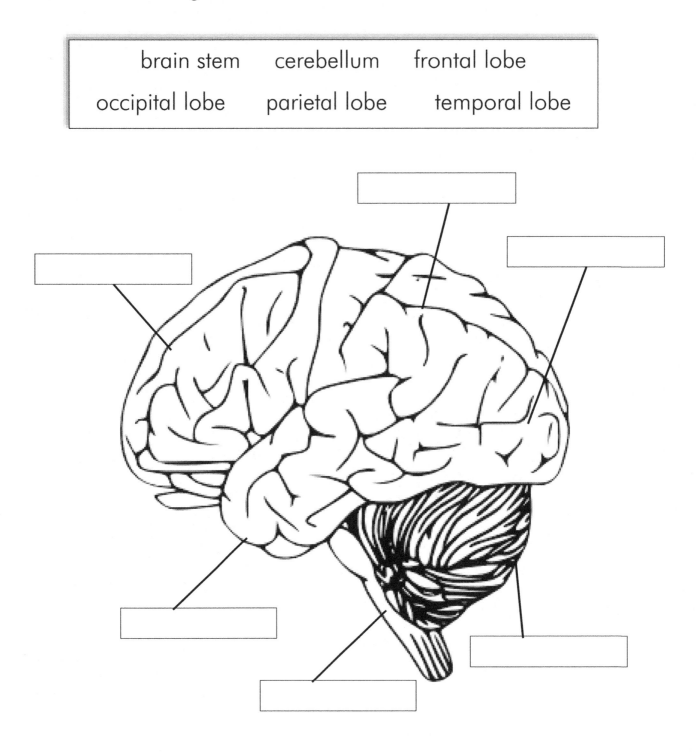

Brain Hat

Follow the directions on the site to make a brain hat.

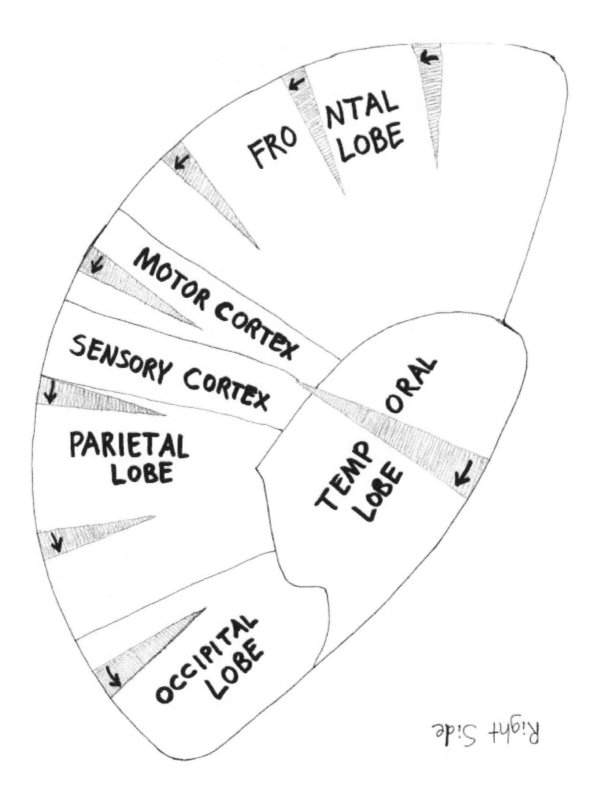

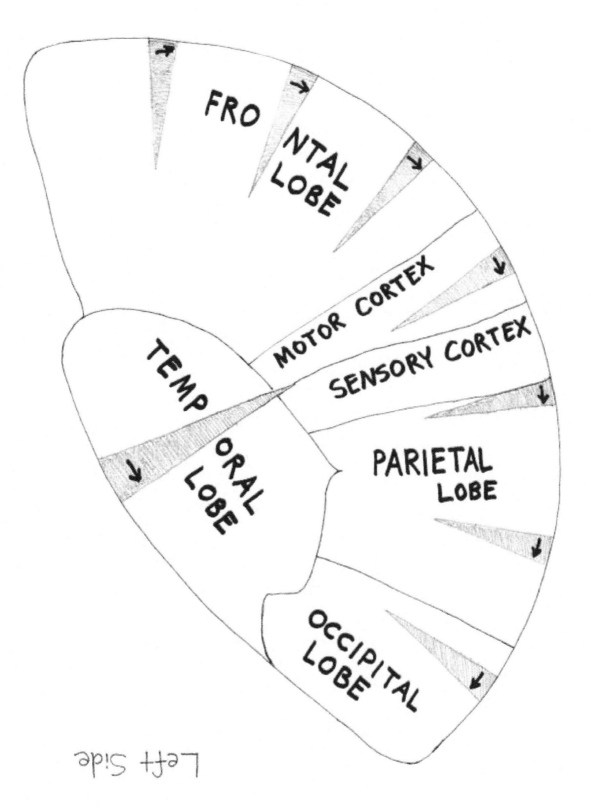

FRONTAL LOBE

MOTOR CORTEX

SENSORY CORTEX

TEMPORAL LOBE

PARIETAL LOBE

OCCIPITAL LOBE

Left Side

Data Chart

Use this data chart to complete your experiment. In the "time" box, record how long it took to find all ten matches.

Trial number	Time
Trial 1	
Trial 2	
Trial 3	
Trial 4	
Trial 5	
Trial 6	

Experiment Worksheet

Fill out this worksheet as you work through the experiment.

Question: _____

Hypothesis: _____

_____

Materials: _____

_____

Procedure: _____

_____

_____

_____

_____

Observations/data: _____

_____

_____

_____

Conclusion: _____

_____

_____

Genetics Activity

First, color in the circles using the directions on the site. Then use your colored-in sheet to answer the questions on the following page.

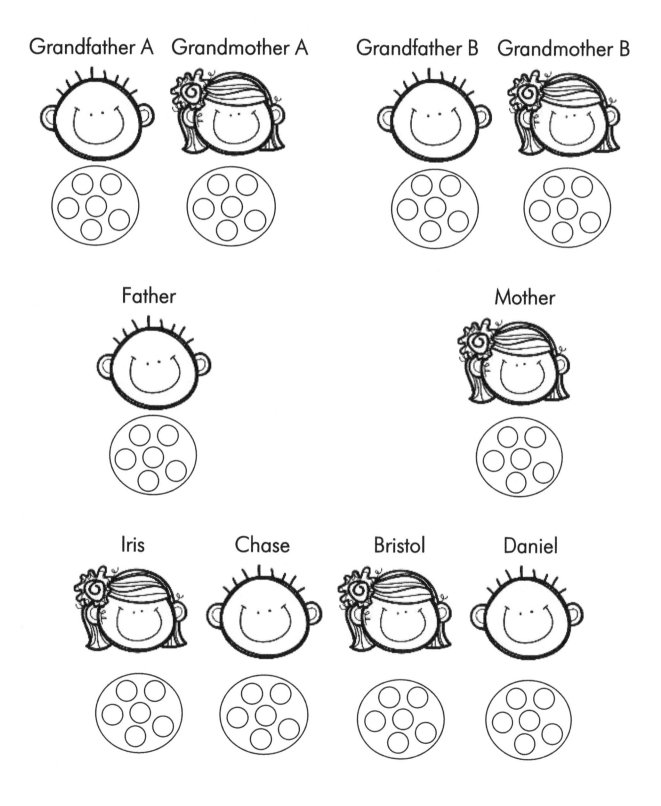

Grandfather A   Grandmother A   Grandfather B   Grandmother B

Father   Mother

Iris   Chase   Bristol   Daniel

Genetics Activity cont.

Use your colored-in sheet to answer the following questions.

1. Do Iris, Chase, Bristol, and Daniel have the exact same traits as their parents, and as each other? In other words, are they identical?

2. Is there variation in the traits the children received?

3. How many of the children at the bottom inherited a trait from each grandparent at the top?

4. Was there any grandparent at the top whose color was not represented in a child at the bottom?

Body Bingo

This page is your body bingo board.

Body Bingo

Body Bingo

Cut out the pieces and arrange them on your board in a random order. There are more pieces than squares for variation purposes.

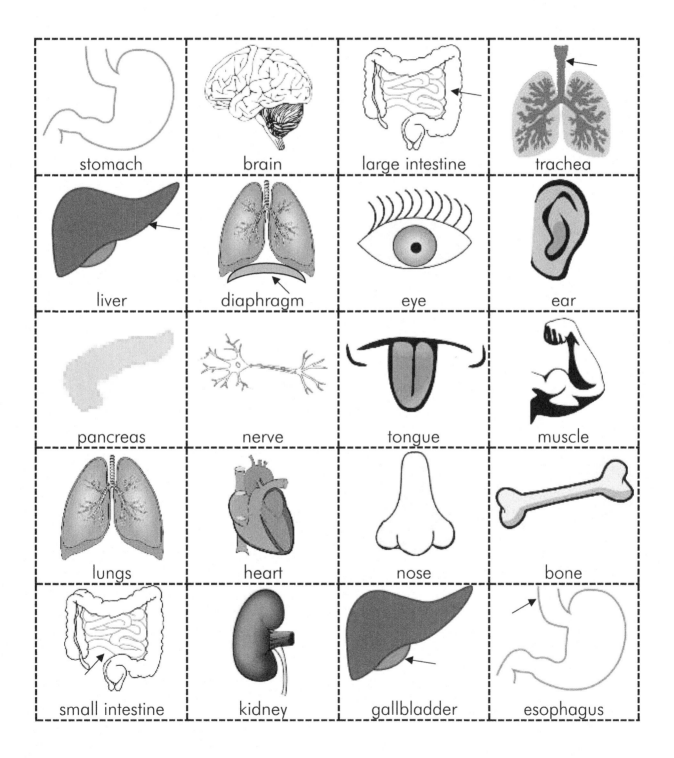

Body Bingo

Have someone read out the questions and see if you have the answer on your bingo board. Can you figure it out without the answer being given to you?

1. This part tells your muscles to move. (brain)

2. This is lined with mucus to protect it from its own acid. (stomach)

3. This part uses peristalsis to move food down. (esophagus)

4. This produces insulin. (pancreas)

5. This organ can't work without light. (eye)

6. Being hit in this muscle knocks the wind out of you. (diaphragm)

7. Uncoiled, this would stretch out over 16 feet. (small intestine)

8. These only contract. (muscles)

9. This body part branches into bronchial tubes. (trachea)

10. This organ includes the vena cava. (heart)

11. The hepatic veins and arteries go in and out of this organ. (liver)

12. The renal veins and arteries go in and out of this organ. (kidney)

13. This connects to both the liver and the stomach. (gall bladder)

14. This body part sits beneath the uvula. (tongue)

15. The alveoli are found here. (lungs)

16. The appendix is attached to this. (large intestine)

17. The brain connects to this part via the auditory nerve. (ear)

18. The space between these is the synapse. (nerves)

19. Blood cells are made inside this. (bone)

20. Tiny hairs allow this organ to filter out dust. (nose)

Word Find

Use the definitions to find the hidden word in the grid. The letters can go any direction around the grid, but will never cross.

D	O	L	M
I	G	P	A
E	S	E	R
V	I	T	S

System responsible for extracting nutrients from food

_____

T	I	M	S
R	S	M	O
E	N	U	F
A	E	T	L

System responsible for fighting disease in the body

_____

S	E	R	P
P	I	R	E
Y	L	A	N
R	O	T	T

System responsible for oxygenation of the body

_____

M	E	O	B
O	H	S	T
C	I	S	A
A	S	F	W

Process by which the body maintains stability

_____

D	I	M	C
G	K	E	Y
L	S	L	F
A	T	E	U

System that protects and supports the body

_____

N	H	V	M
T	C	S	U
E	U	L	G
K	R	A	T

System responsible for allowing the body to move

_____

A	H	D	O
R	C	J	E
K	E	L	X
U	N	L	S

The building blocks of the body

_____

R	C	I	P
E	X	E	L
T	F	B	S
O	R	Y	V

System responsible for removing waste from the body

_____

Q	M	E	N
C	W	R	A
L	G	V	T
Y	J	E	S

Send messages throughout the body

_____

Word Find

Use the definitions to find the hidden word in the grid. The letters can go any direction around the grid, but will never cross.

C	G	A	N
I	R	C	I
Y	B	U	L
R	O	T	A

System responsible for transporting nutrients and waste

_____

I	N	R	O
S	A	G	D
M	T	I	F
C	O	P	E

A living thing

_____

E	I	R	S
B	N	C	O
R	E	N	D
U	T	I	K

Glands that serve to regulate things such as metabolism

_____

T	P	L	N
I	S	E	D
Y	S	U	C
A	R	M	I

Group of cells working Together

_____

D	C	L	F
I	S	J	E
O	A	N	B
R	G	I	R

Group of tissues working together

_____

C	I	Y	S
E	T	S	N
M	R	L	O
G	A	D	E

Group of organs working together

_____

A	S	U	L
T	C	M	I
R	L	E	K
D	P	N	B

Contracts to create movement

_____

N	I	C	O
T	E	G	V
R	Y	U	M
A	T	N	E

System responsible for regulating temperature

_____

V	I	B	R
E	T	C	E
S	U	N	N
L	F	O	C

Tissue that joins things together

_____

Observation Sheet

Use this sheet to record your observations.

Plants	Things that need plants

Compare Elements of Growth

Use this sheet to record your findings.

Day	Light	Dark	Fan
1			
2			
3			
4			
5			
6			
7			
8			
9			
10			
11			
12			
13			
14			

Experiment Worksheet

Fill out this worksheet as you work through the experiment.

Question: _____

Hypothesis: _____

_____

Materials: _____

_____

Procedure: _____

_____

_____

_____

_____

Observations/data: _____

_____

_____

_____

_____

Conclusion: _____

_____

_____

Plant Categories

Write or draw as many examples as you can think of for each category.

Roots	Seeds	Leaves

Fruits	Flowers	Stems

Tree Observation

Sit quietly near your tree. Take notes on your observations.

Draw the tree. Use a tape measure to record the measurement around the tree. _____	**Looking** What living things do you see in and near your tree? **Listening** Do you hear animals playing or singing in the tree? Do you hear wind moving leaves or branches?
Make a rubbing of the bark.	**Touching** Is the bark smooth or rough? Are the leaves soft or prickly?
Make a rubbing or trace a leaf.	**Smelling** What does the bark smell like? The leaves? Are there flowers on the tree?
What season is it now? What kind of tree are you observing?	**Any other observations?** Has the tree changed since the previous season?

Tree Observation

Sit quietly near your tree. Take notes on your observations.

Draw the tree. Use a tape measure to record the measurement around the tree. _____	**Looking** What living things do you see in and near your tree?
	Listening Do you hear animals playing or singing in the tree? Do you hear wind moving leaves or branches?
Make a rubbing of the bark.	**Touching** Is the bark smooth or rough? Are the leaves soft or prickly?
Make a rubbing or trace a leaf.	**Smelling** What does the bark smell like? The leaves? Are there flowers on the tree?
What season is it now? What kind of tree are you observing?	**Any other observations?** Has the tree changed since the previous season?

Scavenger Hunt

Use this page for your scavenger hunt if it is currently fall.

Fall

Look for these:

- A falling leaf
- A crawling insect
- A bird
- 3 different color leaves
- A seed
- A flying insect
- Animal tracks

Colors found: _____

Listen for these:

- Something moved by the wind
- Leaves crunching
- An animal's call
- An insect

What else do you hear?

Touch these:

- A crunchy, crinkly leaf
- A smooth rock
- Tree bark

What did it feel like?

Smell these:

- Campfire
- Pine cones

What else do you smell?

Scavenger Hunt

Use this page for your scavenger hunt if it is currently spring.

Spring

Look for these:

- ❀ Mud
- ❀ A bird
- ❀ A small wildflower
- ❀ Weeds
- ❀ A crawling insect

- ❀ New leaves on a tree
- ❀ A bird's nest
- ❀ A tall wildflower
- ❀ A worm
- ❀ A flying insect

Touch these:

- ❀ A warm, sunny spot
- ❀ A shady, cool spot
- ❀ Flower petals
- ❀ A smooth rock
- ❀ Wet mud
- ❀ Tree bark

What did it feel like?

Listen for these:

- ❀ Something moved by the wind
- ❀ A bird's song/call
- ❀ An animal's call
- ❀ An insect

What else do you hear?

Smell these:

- ❀ A flower
- ❀ Grass

What else do you smell?

Scavenger Hunt

Use this page for your scavenger hunt if it is currently summer.

Summer

Look for these:

☀A bird flying   ☀A bird walking
☀Fruit or berries   ☀Mushroom
☀A crawling insect   ☀A flying insect
☀Something red: _____
☀Something green: _____

Listen for these:

☀A flying insect
☀Something moved by the wind
☀An animal's call

What else do you hear?

Touch these:

☀Something hot from the sun
☀A smooth rock
☀Somewhere cool and shady
☀Tree bark

What did it feel like?

Smell these:

☀A flower
☀Grass

What else do you smell?

Scavenger Hunt

Use this page for your scavenger hunt if it is currently winter.

Winter

Look for these:

- Animal tracks
- An acorn or pinecone
- Berries on a plant
- Trees with no leaves
- A bird
- A feather
- Something with thorns
- Trees with a few leaves

Listen for these:

- An animal's call

What animal did you hear?

- Something moved by the wind

What else do you hear?

Touch these:

- Something wet
- A smooth rock
- Smooth tree bark
- Rough tree bark
- A pinecone

Smell these:

- Hot cocoa!
- A crackling fire

What else do you smell?

Soil Square Observations

Use the boxes to record your observations.

Soil Substitute Observations

Use the boxes to record your observations.

1._____

2._____

3._____

4._____

5._____

6._____

7._____

8._____

9._____

What Did You Learn?

Answer the following questions about the overview you read. Fill in the bubble next to the correct answer. Then label the seed parts at the bottom.

Seeds are made inside a plant's _____.
○ fruit   ○ leaves   ○ stem

The protective covering of a seed is called the _____.
○ hilum   ○ micropyle   ○ seed coat

The scar that shows where a seed was attached to the plant is the _____.
○ micropyle   ○ radicle   ○ hilum

The part of the seed through which pollen enters is the _____.
○ cotyledon   ○ micropyle   ○ radicle

This forms a small root inside the seed.
○ radicle   ○ hilum   ○ cotyledon

This provides food for the new plant as it grows.
○ micropyle   ○ cotyledon   ○ seed coat

Experiment Worksheet

Fill out this worksheet as you work through the experiment.

Question: _____

Hypothesis: _____

_____

Materials: _____

_____

Procedure: _____

_____

_____

_____

_____

Observations/data: _____

_____

_____

_____

_____

Conclusion: _____

_____

_____

Plant Categories

Write one specific type of plant in each category. You can use the internet to help you if you need to.

Angiosperms _____

Sphenopsids _____

Gymnosperms _____

Ferns _____

Bryophytes _____

Algae _____

KWL Chart

Fill in the sections of this chart as you work through the project.

Topic: _____

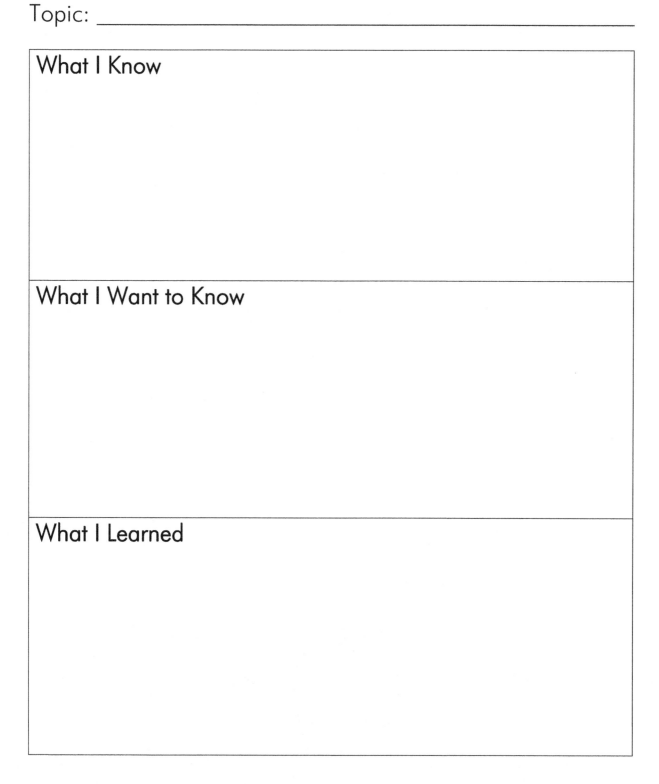

What I Know

What I Want to Know

What I Learned

Reproduction Cartoon

Draw the process from pollen to fruit.

KWL Chart

Fill in the sections of this chart as you work through the project.

Topic: _____

What I Know

What I Want to Know

What I Learned

Mold Observations

Draw pictures or write a description of what you think your food will look like on the given days. Then draw or write what it actually looks like when the days arrive.

Hypothesis	Actual
Day 4	
Day 6	
Day 9	
Day 12	

World Map

Use this world map along with your biome lapbook.

Biome Lapbook

Use these lapbook pieces to record information as you learn about biomes.

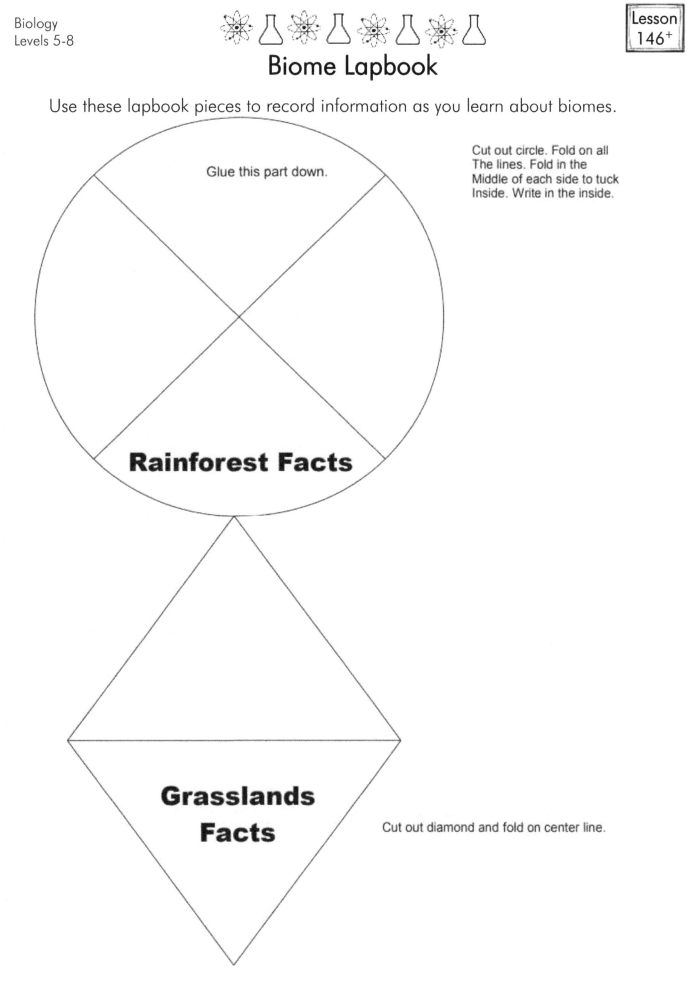

Glue this part down.

Cut out circle. Fold on all
The lines. Fold in the
Middle of each side to tuck
Inside. Write in the inside.

Rainforest Facts

**Grasslands
Facts**

Cut out diamond and fold on center line.

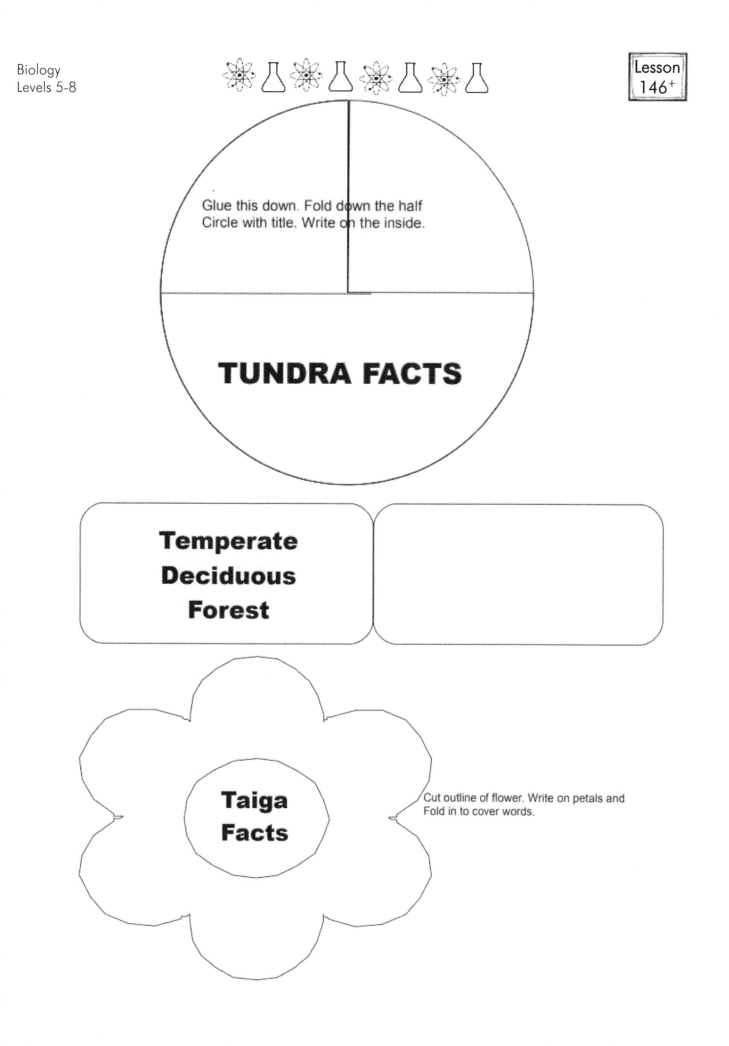

Glue this down. Fold down the half
Circle with title. Write on the inside.

TUNDRA FACTS

**Temperate
Deciduous
Forest**

**Taiga
Facts**

Cut outline of flower. Write on petals and
Fold in to cover words.

Cut out these two rectangles as one piece.
Cut out the gray rectangle on the right.

Cut out the rectangle below with the extra
Edge as one piece. Write your facts on it.
Start under the line.

Place your facts face down so your words
Will show out the window.

Fold this rectangle over and glue along the
Side and bottom. Make sure "Desert facts"
Stick out the top.

Cut out this rectangle.

Glue
Here.

Glue here.

Desert Facts

Scientific Method

Make an observation
Pick something that interests you and observe it closely.
Is there something about it that makes you wonder?

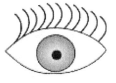

Ask a question
Be specific in your questions about who, what, where, when, why, which, or how. Make sure the questions can be measured with an experiment.

Research the subject
Gather information that pertains to your observation and your question. Begin preparation for your experiment.

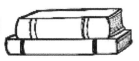

Form a hypothesis
Make an educated guess about what you think will happen in your experiment. Make sure it's something that can be measured by your experiment and that it answers your question.

Conduct the experiment
Detail your materials and instructions. Repeat the process to be sure of your results. Pay attention to variables and only change one at a time to ensure accuracy.

Organize your data
Make a summary of your experiment's results. You can utilize graphs or charts if helpful.

Analyze the results
Determine whether your hypothesis is true. If true, report your findings. If false or partly true, you can retry your experiment with a modified hypothesis.

Report your findings
Share your knowledge with others!

Scientific Method

Fill out the steps of the scientific method on the lines.

1. _____

2. _____

3. _____

4. _____

5. _____

6 _____

7. _____

8. _____

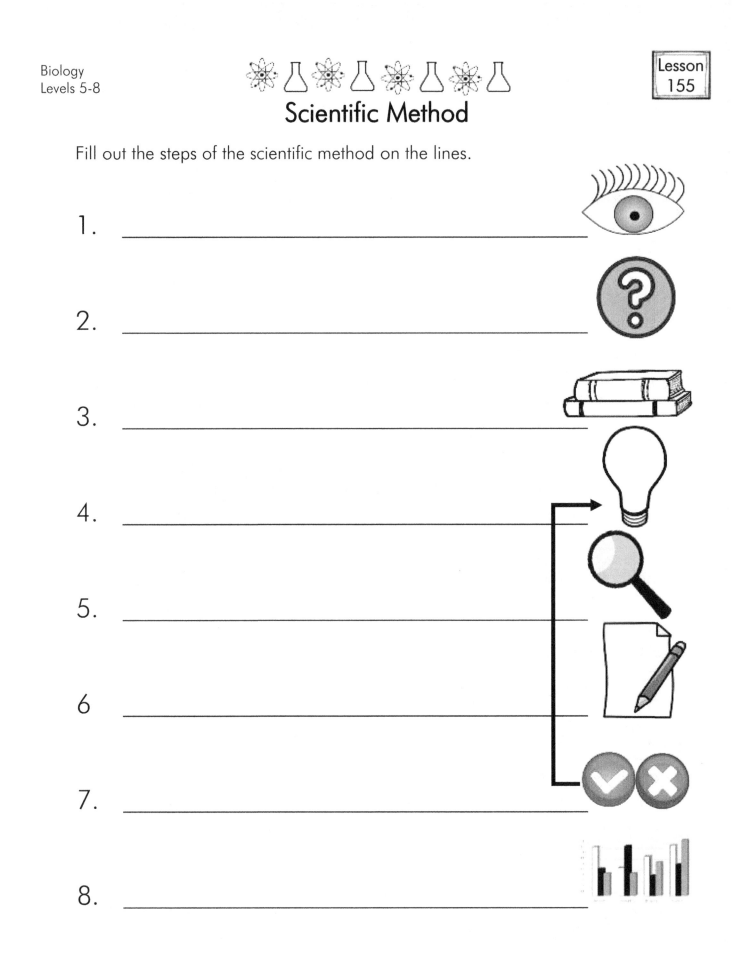

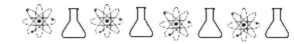
Form a Question

Formulate your question and fill it in here. You can cut out the pieces if you'd like to make a lapbook.

Who?

What?

Where?

When?

Why?

Which?

How?

My Question _____

_____

_____

_____

_____

_____

_____

_____

Research Notes

Use these pages to make notes on your topic.

Topic:_____

Resource 1:_____

Info:_____   Info:_____

Info:_____   Info:_____

Info:_____   Info:_____

Resource 2:_____

Info:_____   Info:_____

Info:_____   Info:_____

Info:_____   Info:_____

Resource 3:_____

Info:_____   Info:_____

Info:_____   Info:_____

Info:_____   Info:_____

Resource 4:_____

Info:_____   Info:_____

Info:_____   Info:_____

Info:_____   Info:_____

Resource 5:_____

Info:_____   Info:_____

Info:_____   Info:_____

Info:_____   Info:_____

Resource 6:_____

Info:_____   Info:_____

Info:_____   Info:_____

Info:_____   Info:_____

Resource 7:_____

Info:_____   Info:_____

Info:_____   Info:_____

Info:_____   Info:_____

Resource 8:_____

Info:_____   Info:_____

Info:_____   Info:_____

Info:_____   Info:_____

Resource 9:_____

Info:_____   Info:_____

Info:_____   Info:_____

Info:_____   Info:_____

Hypothesis and Variables

Use this page to record your hypothesis and variables. You can cut the pieces out if you're making a lapbook.

My Hypothesis: _____

_____

_____

_____

My independent variable(s):

_____

_____

_____

_____

My controlled variable(s):

_____

_____

_____

Variables

Independent:
What I will change

Dependent:
What I will be measuring and observing

Controlled:
What I will keep the same

My Experiment

Use these pages to record your materials and the steps in your experiment. It's okay if you don't fill up all of the space.

My Materials: _____

_____

_____

_____

_____

Steps in My Experiment

Form a Question

Formulate your question and fill it in here. You can cut out the pieces if you'd like to make a lapbook.

Who?

What?

Where?

When?

Why?

Which?

How?

My Question _____

_____

_____

_____

_____

_____

_____

_____

Research Notes

Use these pages to make notes on your topic.

Topic:_____

Resource 1:_____

Info:_____   Info:_____

Info:_____   Info:_____

Info:_____   Info:_____

Resource 2:_____

Info:_____   Info:_____

Info:_____   Info:_____

Info:_____   Info:_____

Resource 3:_____

Info:_____   Info:_____

Info:_____   Info:_____

Info:_____   Info:_____

Resource 4:_____

Info:_____   Info:_____

Info:_____   Info:_____

Info:_____   Info:_____

Resource 5:_____

Info:_____   Info:_____

Info:_____   Info:_____

Info:_____   Info:_____

Resource 6:_____

Info:_____   Info:_____

Info:_____   Info:_____

Info:_____   Info:_____

Resource 7:_____

Info:_____   Info:_____

Info:_____   Info:_____

Info:_____   Info:_____

Resource 8:_____

Info:_____   Info:_____

Info:_____   Info:_____

Info:_____   Info:_____

Resource 9:_____

Info:_____   Info:_____

Info:_____   Info:_____

Info:_____   Info:_____

Hypothesis and Variables

Use this page to record your hypothesis and variables. You can cut the pieces out if you're making a lapbook.

My Hypothesis: _____

_____

_____

_____

My independent variable(s):

_____

_____

_____

_____

Variables

Independent:
What I will change

Dependent:
What I will be measuring and observing

Controlled:
What I will keep the same

My controlled variable(s):

_____

_____

_____

My Experiment

Use these pages to record your materials and the steps in your experiment. It's okay if you don't fill up all of the space.

My Materials: _____

_____

_____

_____

_____

_____

Steps in My Experiment

_____

_____

_____

_____

_____

_____

_____

_____

_____

Tree Observation

Sit quietly near your tree. Take notes on your observations.

	Looking
	What living things do you see in and near your tree?
	Listening
	Do you hear animals playing or singing in the tree? Do you hear wind moving leaves or branches?
Draw the tree. Use a tape measure to record the measurement around the tree. _____	
Make a rubbing of the bark.	Touching
	Is the bark smooth or rough? Are the leaves soft or prickly?
Make a rubbing or trace a leaf.	Smelling
	What does the bark smell like? The leaves? Are there flowers on the tree?
What season is it now? What kind of tree are you observing?	Any other observations?
	Has the tree changed since the previous season?

Made in the USA
Monee, IL
06 September 2020